It's Easy To Play Classics.

Wise Publications
London/New York/Sydney

Exclusive Distributors:
Music Sales Limited
8/9 Frith Street, London, W1V 5TZ, England.
Music Sales Pty. Limited
120 Rothschild Avenue, Rosebery, NSW 2018, Australia.

This book © Copyright 1979 by
Wise Publications
ISBN 0.86001.411.8
Order No. AM 19563

Music Sales complete catalogue lists thousands
of titles and is free from your local music book
shop, or direct from Music Sales Limited.
Please send a Cheque or Postal Order for £1·50 for postage to
Music Sales Limited, 8/9 Frith Street, London, W1V 5TZ.

Printed in England by
Caligraving Limited, Thetford, Norfolk

A Song

Cornelius Gurlitt

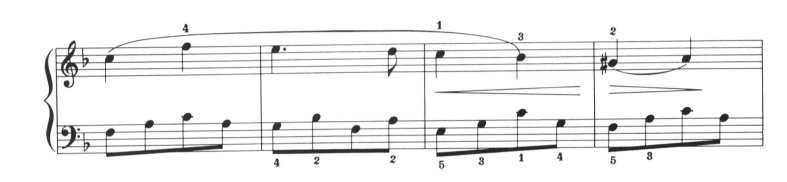

Walking

Antonio Diabelli

Minuet

Henry Purcell

Chorale

Robert Schumann

Robert Schumann
(1810~1856)

In May

Franz Behr

Minuet

Johann Sebastian Bach

Moderato

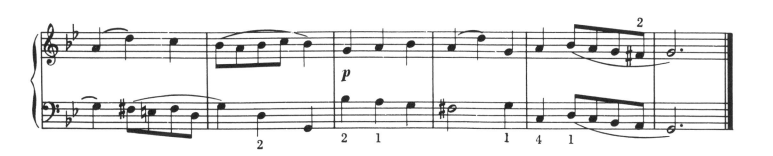

Bourrée

Johann Sebastian Bach

Minuet

Johann Sebastian Bach

Allegretto Scherzando

Carl Phillip Emanuel Bach

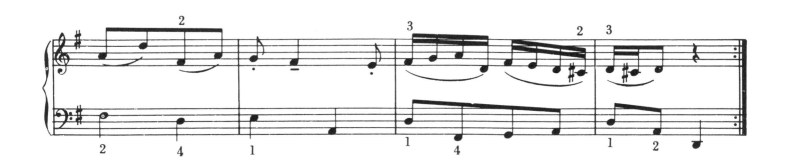

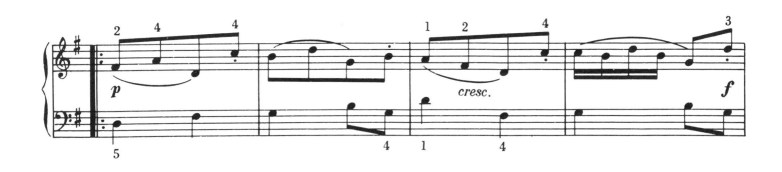

Air

Wilhelm Friedemann Bach

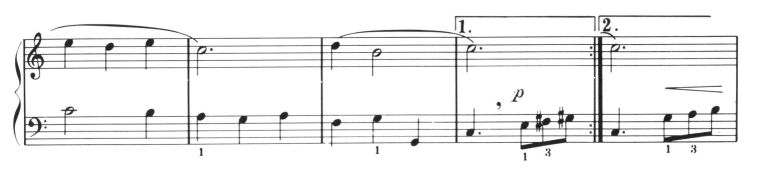

Studio

Johann Christoph Friedrich Bach

Bourrée

Georg Frideric Handel

Gavotte

Georg Frideric Handel

Bourrée

Johann Krieger

Sonata
(Minuet)

Domenico Scarlatti

The Cuckoo

August Eberhard Müller

Arietta

Wolfgang Amadeus Mozart

Sonatina
(Op.57, No.1)

Albert Biehl

Allegro moderato

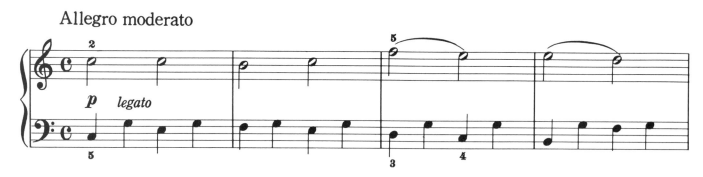

German Dance

Joseph Haydn

Allegretto

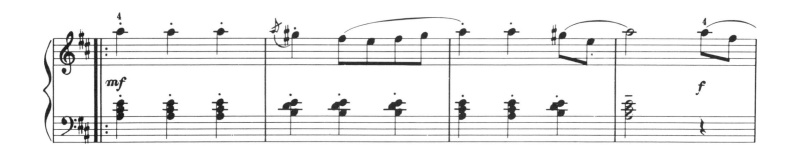

Waltz

Franz Schubert

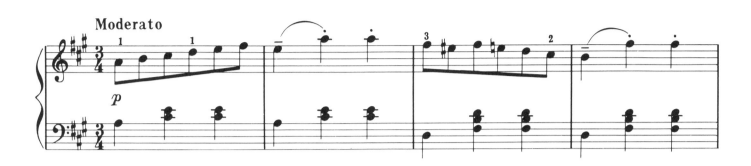

German Dance

Joseph Haydn

D. C. al Fine

Little Fairy Waltz

Ludovic Streabbog

Two Minuets
(Notebook for Nannerl)

Leopold Mozart

Allegretto

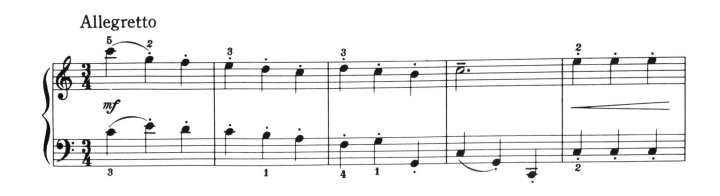

II.

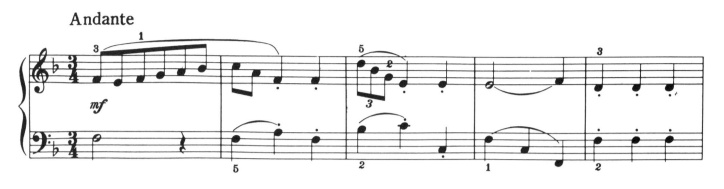

Polka

Mikhail Ivanovich Glinka

The Happy Farmer

Robert Schumann

Blindman's Buff

Robert Schumann

Melody

Robert Schumann

Wedding Marches

Felix Mendelssohn / Richard Wagner

Wedding March — Mendelssohn

Barcarolle
(from "Tales of Hoffmann")

Jacques Offenbach

The Doll's Complaint

César Franck

Evening Star
(from "Tannhaüser")

Richard Wagner

Spring Song

Felix Mendelssohn

Four Scotch Dances

Friedrich Kuhlau

I

II

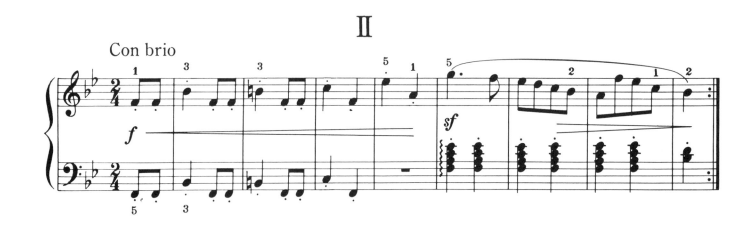

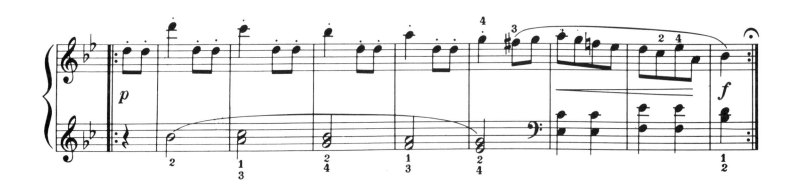

III

Comodo

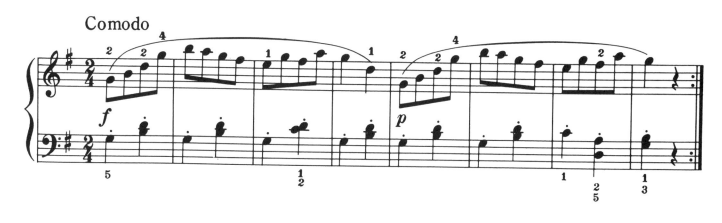

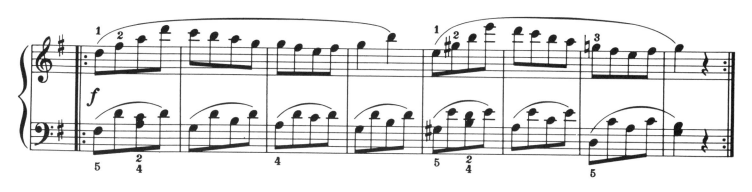

IV

Agitato

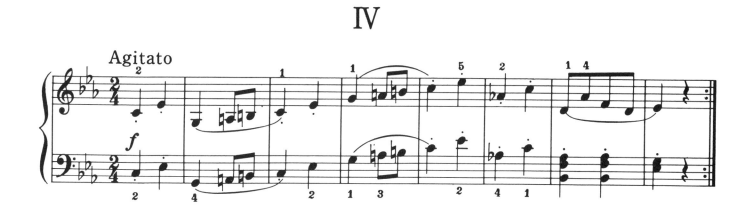

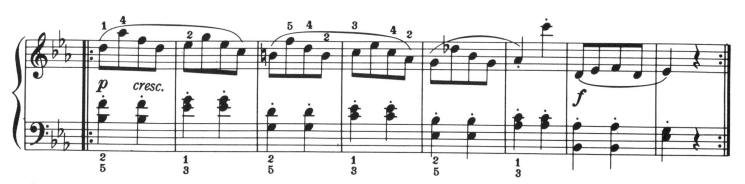

Melody in F

Anton Rubinstein

11(93 (16503)